S A I N T
MAXIMILIAN
K O L B E

The Story of the Two Crowns

Claire Jordan Mohan

YOUNG SPARROW PRESS
P.O. Box 265 • Worcester, PA 19490
(215) 997-0791

Mohan, Claire Jordan
     Saint Maximilian Kolbe — The Story of the Two Crowns

© Copyright 1999
Young Sparrow Press, Box 265, Worcester, PA 19490
(215) 997-0791.
All rights reserved.
Printed in the United States of America.
First Printing.
Cover design and art by Carrie Gamble

ISBN #0-9621500-3-7 $8.95 paperback
Photographs: Catholic News Service
     AP/Wide World Photos

*"The salvation of man is
through love and in love."*

Viktor E. Frankl

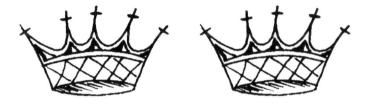

To Maria Teresa, Anne, and Mary Catherine

Saint Maximilian Kolbe

Contents

Francis Gajowniczek
Auschwitz survivor owes his life
to St. Maximilian Kolbe.

1

Christmas Eve

Helena pulled back the heavy velvet drape and looked out the small living room window at the front of the house. She shook her grey curly head in concern. Heavy flakes of white were falling to the ground. The pavement and grass were frosty and the wind was starting to pick up, its howl resounding like a whistle in her ears.

"Oh, Francis, it is starting to snow!" she called to her husband, who was placing a fresh log on the fire. "I do hope the family gets here before it is too heavy."

It was Christmas Eve in Poland and the Gajowniczeks (Ga-yov-nee-check) were preparing for the celebration of Jesus's birth. A tall fir tree stood by the dining room awaiting the decorations made last week by their nieces and nephews. On a table nearby lay paper cutouts of angels, ornaments fashioned of colored paper, multi-colored ribbons, and gay ornaments of beads and empty egg shells. The children had had such fun making them. It had been a special Advent night spent with their grand-aunt and uncle and an activity that they looked forward to all year.

Yesterday, while the gingerbread men were baking in the oven, Helena had tied apples on colored strings and wrapped nuts in gold and silver foil. Francis told her they glistened like the Magi's jewels. Everything was ready for the tree trimming and she hoped the bad weather would not interfere.

She went into the kitchen to lower the oven. Dinner was almost ready. "Ah, the 'wigilia' (vee-gill-yah) is my favorite supper of the whole year," she thought to herself. "It is such a happy time."

Several automobiles stopped outside, the sound of the motors was like a melody to her ears. As the car doors slammed, she smiled. She put down the spoon with which she had been tasting the soup and removed her apron. Excited voices reached her as the front door was thrown open. She rushed in to greet her sisters and brothers and all their children, her plump arms surrounding them with strong hugs.

As she pressed the little children to her bosom, Helena felt a fleeting moment of sadness as she thought of her own two boys no longer with them, killed by the Germans during World War II. Briefly, tears filled her eyes. No matter how many years passed her heart still ached for them. If only she had children and grandchildren of her own! Then, as her eyes fell upon her dear husband, sitting in his favorite chair, smoking his pipe, she wiped her eyes. Silently, she thanked God for the miracle that saved him. What would she have done without her Francis!

"Welcome, welcome," she pronounced warmly, "We

were so afraid you wouldn't make it with snow coating the roads."

The guests brushed off their clothes and removed their boots as Francis, grabbing his cane, rose from his easy chair to embrace each one.

"Give me your coats and hats," he said. Carefully, he placed them on the coat rack.

"Now, gentlemen, let us sit by the fire and get warm. Helena and the ladies have things to do in the kitchen."

The women filed into the dining room to set the table.

"Everything smells great," said her sister, "and I remembered the hay; I got it from the barn the first thing this morning."

Turning to her little grandson, she gave him a kiss and added, "We must remember the baby Jesus' birth in the manger. Now, little Paul, come help me spread some hay over the table."

The little tot smoothed the blades with his tiny hands so that his Aunt Helena could cover the table with her finest linen cloth and put out the sparkling dishes and silverware.

"And don't forget to set an extra place," cautioned the little boy. "A stranger might stop by tonight."

Meanwhile, the other little cousins, happy to see each other, were chattering away. They could hardly wait to decorate the tree with the many sparkling ornaments they had made.

"Come, Aunt Helena, Uncle Francis. Come, Grandma. We'll make this year's tree the prettiest ever," they called to the elders.

With that they all marched into the parlor and placed the ornaments on the fir's thick branches. When it was finished, they all cheered as the tallest boy placed a glimmering star on top.

"It is beautiful," applauded their parents.

"Oh, so lovely. Children, you did a wonderful job," whispered Francis as he leaned forward to put his arms around to embrace them.

The evening sky had darkened. The little ones ran to the window.

"It's time to watch the sky," called the girls, each one hoping to be the first to see the "gwiazdka," (g'vee-azd-kah) the little star.

Little Frania jumped up and down as she shouted, "I see it! I see it! I see the "gwiazdka!" Though they smiled at her joy, they all knew the snow was really hiding it from her eyes.

Hugging and kissing her, the children clapped their hands and walked to the dining room where supper was waiting. The whole family looked forward to this meal which they called "wigilia." Tonight, there would be eleven special dishes. As soon as they sat down and said their grace, Francis broke the Christmas wafer (the oplatwk [oh-pwah-tek]) giving it first to his wife and then from the oldest person present to the youngest, wishing them "Happy Christmas Holidays." Then the feast began!

Afterwards, filled with wild mushroom soup, carp, coffee cake and many other delicious foods, Francis led them into the living room to sing carols before it was time for Midnight Mass.

When the singing had finished, they sat quietly for a few moments, thinking of Christmases past — each with his own recollections.

The solemn silence was broken by Peter. "Uncle Francis," he said as he looked at the little table with lit candles and a framed picture standing in a bright corner of the room, "Tell us the story again. Tell us how your life was saved when you were in the concentration camp."

"And," added Joseph, "tell us all about Maximilian Kolbe. Tell us about when he was a little boy. Was he brave even then?"

Francis silently contemplated the face in the frame—a monk who gave up his life to save him. Tears rolled down his wrinkled cheeks like tiny rivulets on his furrowed face. How could he ever thank that man, and God, who had given him the happiness he shared with his family this night—and all through the years.

He smiled at the little boys and girls who looked at him expectantly. They had heard the story many times. "Well," he began, "I was saved the first week of August in 1941, but the story really began many years before that. It is the story of a little boy who loved the Madonna and somehow always knew the way he would die..."

2

A Little Boy

Francis settled into his comfortable chair by the fire. The children circled him as they sat on the floor. Francis began...

There once was a little boy, much like you children. He was born over a hundred years ago on January 8, 1894. His mother's name was Maria and his father's name was Jules. He was the second of three boys in the family. His brother, Francis, was a year and a half older and his brother, Joseph, was two years younger. Since they were close in age, they were also close in spirit and had a lot of good times together.

His parents were very good and holy people. In fact, his mother had always wanted to be a religious sister, but since her family was poor, they had no money for a dowry. Since this was not possible, Maria prayed that God would send her a good husband who did "not curse or drink, or go to the tavern with his friends."

God answered her prayer when she was twenty years old and she met Jules. He was a very good Catholic man who had all the qualities she wanted. They fell in love and were married on October 5, 1891.

This couple lived in a cottage in the village of Zdunska-Wola (Zz-doon-skah Voll-ah) in Poland. It was very small—just one room. They had a kitchen and a workshop big enough to hold a loom and behind a curtain, they had beds and a bureau. Since Jules was a weaver this was perfect for him. Later, they moved to a bigger home where Maria had a little store. She sold various things that her neighbors would need, sort of like a 5¢ and 10¢ or Dollar store that we have today.

They were a happy little family who loved Jesus and his mother Mary very much. One warm Sunday when the boys were still little, they all traveled to the Shrine of Our Lady of Czestochowa (Chen-sto-ho-vah). On the way, Jules and Maria had made an important decision. When they arrived in the church, they knelt before the statue of Our Lady.

"Dear Madonna," they prayed. "We are a poor, but happy couple. We love you and your Son, Jesus. We have been blessed with three dear sons and we want to dedicate our oldest to you. We don't have much money now, but we will work very hard and save every penny so that Francis can have a good education and become a priest."

They blessed themselves and journeyed home with joy in their hearts feeling God was pleased with them. They wanted the best for all three boys, but in those days only people with money could afford to give their children a good education. The younger boys would not need to go to high school, the parents reasoned. They would follow in their father's footsteps as weavers and farmers and they could serve God in other ways. As for Raymond and Joseph, they were just little kids enjoying life and it didn't occur to them to disagree with their parents. Little did they all know that fate would intervene and make a new choice for them.

This father and mother loved them and, like all parents, wanted the best for them. Jules thought it important that his sons grow up physically healthy and strong, but his way of raising them would seem severe to children today. He wanted to prepare them for life and its hardships. One of his traditions took place each year as soon as the first snow had fallen.

"Come on, boys," he would call, "take off your shoes. We'll have a barefoot race in the garden."

Shivering in advance, they would obey. The garden was large and they would run from one end to the other many times. Even though their feet were frozen, they would not say a word—and they did learn to endure hardship. Perhaps unknowingly, Raymond was being prepared for the suffering he would endure in his later life.

Maria taught them to be mannerly and kind. But in spite of this, Raymond was not always the perfect little boy. Although he was obedient and helpful around the house most of the time, he had a fiery disposition and was sometimes quite obstinate and often spiteful. Even though he would grow up to be a saint, he was not always a saintly little boy!

Back in those days, if you were naughty your parents would spank you with a switch, something unheard of by boys and girls today who are usually punished by the removal of privileges. It was not a pleasant experience and it really hurt! Some children would run and hide when the words, "Bring me the switch," were mentioned. But if Raymond knew he deserved to be beaten, without waiting for his father's command, he would bring the switch and lie down on the bench to take his punishment. Then, unbelievably, hiding his tears, he would thank his parents and put the switch back in place hanging on the wall.

Can you imagine that happening to you today? You can see from this that Raymond was the kind of kid who knew he had to "take his medicine" and he did it bravely.

At school, he was gentle and well-behaved. The teachers were pleased with him. But like all children at some point in their lives, there were times when he was teased by his friends. They gave him a nickname — "Marmalade." Naturally, Ray did not like to be made fun of and most likely had a few fights to prove he was not soft as jelly!

3

The Apparition

Helena interrupted the story with a huge plateful of honey cakes. "Here is a little treat, children," she pronounced. The boys and girls quickly jumped up, eager for one of their favorite things. Francis took a puff on his pipe, waited for the munching to stop, and continued...

When Raymond was ten years old, something special and mysterious happened to him that would change his life. One day he got into trouble—what he did, I don't know—but it must have been very serious for his mother scolded him severely and said, "Raymond, who knows what will become of you!"

His mother forgot all about this incident. Raymond was her little boy, she loved him, and she was not really worried about his behavior, but Raymond thought about this for days. What would become of him? Was he really a bad boy? What should he do? He went to church and prayed to Mary as hard as he could.

"Dear Mother," he prayed, "What will become of me? Will I grow up to be an evil man? Help me to be good."

Even though he felt better after this, he could not forget his mother's remarks. They really troubled him. He tried his best to be good, helping around the house and being obedient. For days he persevered. Even his parents noticed a difference in him. The next week he stopped in church again on his way home from school. His concerns were still plaguing him. He was alone in the little chapel so he opened his heart to God again.

It was then that the Madonna appeared to him. Raymond could hardly believe what he saw. Was he seeing things, he wondered. As he stared at this beautiful lady spellbound, he saw Mary holding two crowns in her hands—one white and one red.

She looked at him kindly and asked, "Dear Raymond, you cannot know what the future will bring, but I am asking you, do you want these two crowns? The white one means that you will remain pure, and the red one means you will be a martyr."

The little boy did not fully understand. How could he? But he gazed at her with love while tears filled his eyes. He knew he wanted to be good and always be close to Jesus and His Blessed Mother.

"Oh yes, dear Mother," he answered, "whatever God asks, I will do."

With that the Madonna looked at him sweetly and disappeared. Ray stayed on his knees a long time thinking about what had happened.

Who would believe him? He left the church a scared and puzzled little boy. He went home, but he said nothing to anyone about what had happened.

Upstairs near his room, there was a small hidden altar where he would often go to pray without letting anyone else see him. He bought a little statue of the Madonna and placed it there. Each day, he knelt before it and remembered what the Blessed Mother had said. One day, as he prayed he began to cry. His mother, passing through the hall, saw him and knew something was very wrong. She went quickly to him and took him in her arms.

"Honey, what is the matter with you?" she asked. "Are you sick? You haven't been yourself lately. Come on, Ray, you must tell mama all about it."

The troubled boy wiped his eyes, and looked up at his mother.

"Oh, Mama, I have something to tell you," shaking and crying at the same time, he blurted out his secret.

"When you scolded me, Mama, I became worried and scared. I prayed very hard to the Madonna and asked her to tell me what would become of me and this is what happened."

He told her about his visit to church and the Madonna's appearance. His mother hugged him to her.

"Oh, Raymond," she said. "You are not a bad boy. I love you and Jesus does, too. Mary has given you a message, but we must not worry about it now."

She wiped his tears away and comforted him. "When you are older, we will understand. You are just a little boy, Ray. For now you must just have faith in God, try your best, and He will show you the way."

From that time on, Raymond seemed changed—no longer obstinate or spiteful, full of kindness— and he did not speak of it again. Yet, his mother wondered what it all meant and she, too, kept the secret.

4

A Student

After his mother consoled him, Raymond was very happy and full of joy and never gave his parents trouble again. Though he was only ten years old, his parents both noticed he seemed like a different boy. He became gentle and prayerful and a devoted altar boy. He loved being in church and was glad when it was his turn to serve at Mass.

Someday, we know he would prove his brave heart, but for now he learned of courageous deeds from books. He loved to read. One of his favorite stories was the life of St. Francis Assisi which his father had given him. He read it over and over—fascinated by the tales of Francis' experiences with birds and animals.

One day, while outside playing beneath a cherry tree filled with chirping birds, he spoke to his next door neighbor who was working on his garden, "I wonder what they're saying. Mr. Pisalski (Pee-sal-ski), wouldn't it be neat if we could speak to the birds like St. Francis did."

"Ah, yes, Ray," was the kind reply, "it would be something if we could. I'll bet they could tell us a lot about the world."

Though this showed his gentleness, Raymond had another side to his character. He greatly admired bravery in the followers of St. Francis. He knew someday he would do great deeds, maybe, be a saint, too! He often went to the Franciscan Friary which was near his home. There he learned about Father Raphael Chylinski, a former officer in the Polish Army, a hero who showed compassion to the victims of war and Brother Angelo Tancredi who also was a noble officer serving his country.

Both had exchanged the sword for the habit—they left the army to serve God. Raymond was held spellbound by the stories of these two brave men and longed to be like them. He thought of his vision of the two crowns and felt somehow there was a connection to the Madonna here and he was destined for the sacrifices and glory of the military life. He could not suspect what the future held for him.

Although the plans were for his brother, Francis, to be the only one educated, Raymond was a smart and studious boy. He was most helpful to his mother and because of this, his intelligence was discovered by a stranger and another change developed in his young life.

One day his mother called him as he sat in his room reading.

"Raymond, come down, I want you to hurry to the drug store. I need medicine for one of my patients."

Maria not only ran a store, she also was a midwife for her neighbors. (In those days when women had their babies at home, this was a lady who was there to help them when the child was born.) Obediently, Ray dashed down the steps and at his mother's direction, he sped to the village store and asked for "Vencon greca."

The pharmacist asked him, "How do you know it is called 'Vencon greca?'"

"That is its Latin name," Ray answered.

"And how do you know Latin?"

"We learn Latin from the priest."

"There's something about this boy," the pharmacist thought. He proceeded to ask the lad a lot of questions about himself—his name, his address, his schooling.

"Oh, Mr. Kotowski, I am not going to high school," Raymond told him. "You see, only my brother is being educated. He will be a priest. My little brother and I will stay at home and work with our papa."

"You have a good mind, lad. I can see that. You must not waste it," said the pharmacist. "I would like to help you. Ask your parents if I may tutor you, then you will be able to go to school with your brother."

Ray took the medicine in his hand and hurried home, quietly pondering the pharmacist's words. He knew he loved learning, but what would his parents say to all this? Later that evening while they were eating supper, he told his papa and mama what had happened.

"Raymond, let us think about this tonight," said his father. "Tomorrow we'll talk to Mr. Kotowski. It is something to consider, but it will be a sacrifice for us."

"Yes," said his mother. "We had not planned on this. But, Jules, perhaps it is the Madonna speaking to us."

The next day, the three of them visited the pharmacy.

"Your son has a great mind. I would be proud to work with him," said the pharmacist.

Since they felt God was intervening with their plans, they agreed and hours were set for Ray's lessons. In no time, he reached the same level as his brother and they were promoted together.

"Oh, I am so happy," Raymond told his parents. "I can now go to business school with Francis."

Though he did not know it, he moved a step closer to his destiny.

5

The Seminary

The grandfather clock struck ten. Uncle Francis glanced about him. Some of the little ones were squirming and little Frania and Lottie were fast asleep curled up like little kittens in the corner. He got up and stretched. His old limbs needed movement!

"Children, it is getting late, and we have been sitting for a long time. Let's get a cup of Auntie's hot chocolate and maybe we'll finish the story tomorrow."

"No, no," they replied. "Please tell us the whole story tonight before church. Let's have our cocoa quickly and then, we promise we'll sit still and be quiet."

Helena poured the drinks which they gulped down before returning to their spot before the fire. Francis pushed his thinning white hair from his eyes, patted their heads kindly, and returned to the story.

"Now, let me see, where was I? Oh, yes, I remember I told you that Raymond was going to be tutored by the pharmacist..."

Raymond did study very hard and in the fall, he was accepted into the "business school"—which we would call high school.

The following year when Raymond was thirteen years old another turning point came into his life. On Easter Sunday, the Kolbe family attended a mission at his church, preached by Franciscan fathers. At the end of the final prayers, just as they were getting up to leave, the priest turned to the congregation.

"My dear people," he announced, "just one moment. I have wonderful news for you. We are opening a new seminary soon and we will welcome any of you young men who would be willing to dedicate your life to the Lord..."

Raymond listened to every word. It seemed the priest was speaking directly to him. Turning to his mother, he exclaimed, "Mama, I must be a missionary. I know this is the crown the Madonna spoke of! Mama, Papa, please may I go talk to the priest?"

His brother, who always knew he was destined to be a priest, chimed in, "Yes, Ray, I think this is right for both of us. Papa, Mama, may we go together?"

Their parents looked at each other and nodded their heads.

"Jules, I think this is what we have been waiting for," said Maria. "God is giving us a message."

As soon as the priest left the altar, the two boys, followed by their parents, ran to the sacristy to talk to the missionary.

"Father, we would like to enter the seminary. We are ready to consecrate ourselves to Jesus," they stated together.

The priest questioned them further and liked what he heard.

"Of course you must finish this year at your school. If you do well, you may join us in the fall," replied the priest.

Turning to Jules and Maria, he added, "With your permission, we will certainly be happy to have two such fine young men."

October came quickly and it was time for them to leave. Their dad took them to the city of Krakow where he put them on the train to complete the journey alone.

"Now, my sons, be good," he begged them, "and study hard. Write to us every week on that paper mama gave you. You know mama and I are very proud of you, but will miss you very much."

He needn't have worried, especially about his younger son whose professors were impressed with his intelligence in science and math. Although his goal was to eventually become a member of the religious community, his professor in mathematics felt this was a mistake.

"It is a pity that this young man, so richly gifted should become a priest," he remarked to another of the teachers.

Meanwhile, the young student was always smiling and friendly. He was an enthusiastic and kind kid who had lots of friends. Other students turned to him for help with the most difficult problems and he was always ready to assist or teach them. His teachers found him to be always obedient, thoughtful, and holy. In his free time, he was often found kneeling before a crucifix alone in prayer.

Raymond was happy at the seminary, but after three years he had to make a choice about entering the novitiate to study to be a priest. He was not so sure this was right for him and was tempted to change his mind. He prayed all the time to the Madonna whom he called "Mamina" to let him know on what battlefield he would earn the two crowns she had shown him

One day, bowing before the altar during Mass, he promised Mary that he would fight for her. Although at that time he did now know how he was to do this, he thought his "battle" would be a bloody one. These thoughts made him hesitate to join the Franciscan order. He felt the military career was what the Lady wanted of him.

When it came time to make the big decision, he was overcome by doubt. It was the night before he would be accepted into the order and he had to know. What should he do? He wanted to be a soldier. His whole family was patriotic. His favorite game was chess and he had launched military campaigns with the wooden pawns. Finally, he came to the conclusion that he couldn't take the religious habit! He convinced his brother Francis to go along with him and they made an appointment to talk to the Superior. Both Francis and Raymond would refuse to enter.

The next morning, just as they were waiting outside the Superior's office, the door bell rang. They were called to the parlor where their mother greeted them with a big hug. After lots of conversation about their dad and Joseph and life at home, she put her arms around them and smiled happily though there were tears in her eyes.

"Boys, there is something I must tell you," she said, "I hope you will understand and be happy for me—I am planning to enter a convent and papa is going to join the Franciscans just like you!"

They stared at her in disbelief!

"Oh, mama!" was all that they could say.

They talked for a long time after that. What else she told them I don't know, but the conversation was enough to change their minds. The two boys decided to stay. After she left, they kept the appointment with the Superior. Although a few years later, Francis did leave to join the army in World War I, Raymond lost his doubts permanently and was soon known as Friar Maximilian.

Marie Dabrowska Kolbe

6

Unusual Parents

The children all looked at Uncle Francis. What had they heard? It didn't make sense!
"Uncle Francis, wait a minute. What do you mean his mother became a religious sister?" asked Adele. "Mothers can't be sisters!"
"Well," responded Francis, "before I tell you the rest of Raymond's story, I'll explain what happened to his parents. Remember I told you in the beginning that Maria always wanted to be a sister, but couldn't when she was young?" He continued...

You see, after Francis and Raymond left home, their younger brother Joseph also wanted to serve Jesus. When he was thirteen, he followed in their footsteps and joined the Franciscan Order. Maria and Jules, alone at home, made a decision. She would now be able to consecrate herself to God as a sister and her husband could be a lay brother. I know this sounds strange to you, but the Church allows this to happen if both the husband and wife agree to this new way of life.

So Raymond's father sold his business and entered a Franciscan Monastery. After a while, he found that at his age he couldn't get used to this way of life. He eventually left and opened a religious gift shop. When World War I started in 1914, he enlisted in the Polish Army and was sent to fight on the Russian Front. He was captured by the enemy and was sentenced to hang. Jules was only forty-three years old when gave his life for his country!

Maria, though, became a very dedicated and loving religious sister. She remained one for the rest of her life—and she lived till she was seventy-six. She was a very good and holy woman who loved Jesus and his Blessed Mother. She was very kind to the poor. All of her free time was spent in church praying. Though she had always been a loving mother, her dream had been to be a sister and now it had come true.

Even though she was in the convent, Maria always stayed close to her boys by writing letters and visiting them. Through the years she was always part of their lives.

She was still a mother, just like yours, who loved her sons very much. You can imagine how much she suffered when she lived to see her youngest boy, Joseph, die of pneumonia in 1930; and Raymond and Francis both die in German concentration camps in World War II.

So you see, Raymond had a very unusual family—each one of them devoted to Jesus and to Mary—and each one of them served God and their country. No wonder Raymond himself was so brave and courageous. The Blessed Lady and the two crowns were always a part of him. And it was only at the end of his life that he finally understood what they meant.

7

A Young Friar

"Uncle Francis," asked Paul, "why is Raymond now called Friar Maximilian?"

"Well, Paul," replied his uncle, "In those days when a man or woman decided to become a Sister or a Brother, they would choose a new name to signify that they were like a new person before God."

"But Maximilian is a strange name," mentioned Peter. "Why did he take that name?"

"I don't really know, what do you think?" answered Francis.

"I have been studying history," spoke up Paul, "and there was a Maximilian who became an admiral of the Austrian navy. He fought with the French army against the Mexicans who wanted their independence. He was captured and shot to death in 1867. He was a brave soldier. Do you think Raymond wanted to be like him?"

"You may have something there," said Francis nodding his head and placing some tobacco in *his pipe. "Raymond always felt he was destined for the military, and remember, he promised to battle for Our Lady, but, of course, we are only guessing about this. Perhaps there was a Saint Maximilian that we have not heard of. Maybe you could check it on your computer tomorrow. Let us go on with his story now. It is getting late..."*

Maximilian was eighteen years old when he became a friar. The good students who were accepted by the Franciscans were sent to Rome to study at the Gregorian University and he was one of the boys chosen. At first, this young innocent Polish boy refused to leave—he was afraid to go to Rome! Other students had hinted that Rome was an evil city! He had heard that women followed even young priests and that the men hated the religious brothers and sisters. How could he keep his "white crown" and his promises to Our Lady in such a place?

His Superiors ordered him to go and since this new friar had made his vow of "obedience," he had to accept. He sat at his desk and wrote to his mother, asking her to pray for his protection. He went to Rome and after a few weeks, his mother received another letter. This time it read, "Don't worry, Mother, ...life here is not as bad as I feared. The Italians have better things to do than bother us."

Time passed and the once fearful young man became used to life in Rome. He studied hard and in his spare time visited its many churches and even the Coliseum where early martyrs had died for their faith—and he continued to feel close to his Blessed Mother.

An interesting thing happened to him during that time. His finger was abscessed and when he went to the doctor he got bad news. The bone was infected and an operation was necessary. He was going to lose his finger! As arrangements were being made, he reached into his pocket and felt a small bottle which his rector had given him.

"Doctor," he said, "I have a little Lourdes water which I received as a souvenir just the other day. I have it right here."

The doctor looked at the frightened boy and thought about this for a few minutes. He prayed silently, then said, "Son, I think we should use it on your finger."

They poured the water and together they prayed to Mary. Maximilian was admitted to the hospital. The next morning dawned and the patient was prepared for the operating room. Before surgery, the doctor came to his bed and inspected the finger. He looked suddenly at the nervous young man, then to the nurse who was assisting him. Kolbe was startled to hear the physician say, "I can't believe it—no surgery is necessary, this boy is completely cured!"

They all fell to their knees in prayer. After this, he became even more devoted to the Blessed Mother. He seemed to have no fear of anything in life. His friends said he saw the Virgin Mary everywhere and difficulties nowhere!

Maximilian was ordained a priest and returned to Poland, but other serious health problems came into his life. One day while playing soccer, he suddenly suffered a hemorrhage and felt blood come to his mouth. He lay down on the grass and blood flowed for a long while. A doctor was called who said his sickness was tuberculosis. This was the beginning of many years of hospitals and rest. Maximilian himself felt he was going to die by the time he was twenty-three. But this young priest still had much work to do before his time was up!

He was sent to a sanatarium where rest was considered the only cure. He was told to walk only a little and slowly. But Maximilian was a priest, and remember, he had been prepared for tough times way back when his father took the boys to the garden. Regardless of the doctor's orders, day and night he ran through the snow and against the wind, his hands like ice, to bring the sacraments to the dying.

After many years, Maximilian finally was cured. He was a true man of God. He followed St. Francis of Assisi by always being good to the poor and the sick, and living a simple life. I don't think he ever spoke to the birds, but he spoke to many people no matter where he went— whether in church, or on trains, or on the street.

Like Jesus, he had the power and charisma that made others listen. He told them about God and the Blessed Mother and convinced them to have faith.

He was guided to found the City of Mary (Niepokolanow) where he published a newspaper called *The Knight of the Immaculata.* This paper, devoted to Mary, was very important to him all his life and was read by people all over the world. When this young priest was sent to Japan and India as a missionary, it was translated into these languages so even people in the Orient were inspired by it.

But eventually, World War II sent Maximilian in a new direction. It was his final turning point! He was forty-five and he had two years left to live. These last days would be totally different from all that went before.

Catholic News Service

Auschwitz

8

World War II

Francis stopped and looked at the children kindly. Tears filled his eyes. His voice shook and he found it hard to go on.

"Children, how can I tell you about war? You, whose lives have never been touched by it, who live at a time of peace; you may hear of sadness and suffering on the news, but how could you fathom what life was like for us during World War II?"

Adolf Hitler was a cruel man who came into power in Germany in 1934. He established what was called a Nazi state. Labor unions were abolished, strikes were forbidden. Economic developments solved the unemployment problems and the average German worker enjoyed posterity. Because of this, people believed in him and no one could deny that the Nazis had engineered the economic recovery of their country.

After Hitler had succeeded in helping his own country, he decided Germany should unite with Austria and other Germanic peoples in central and eastern

Europe. He felt that people of common background, culture, and language should be governed by their peers. He began his campaign in March 1938 when he took Austria by force. Next was the Czech government. The Czechs fought back, but by March 1939, Hitler had swallowed up that country, too. Although Great Britain and France declared war on September 3, 1939, it was too late for Poland.

On September 1, German armies crossed the Polish frontier and launched an attack which immediately shattered the fragile peace. The German tanks were met by the Polish cavalry. Though the Poles were brave, what could horses do against tanks? The use of calvary in modern warfare was inadequate against this new technology of death. By the end of the second week, the Polish army ceased to exist.

On September 5, the German air force bombed Warsaw. Though Niepoklanow (Knee-pokah-lah-nuff) where Father Kolbe's monastery was located, was not far away, it suffered little damage. But the Franciscan community of six or seven hundred religious of the largest monastery in the world were ordered to leave. About forty of the brothers refused and stayed with their superior, Father Kolbe. They wondered what their fate would be.

Two weeks later they found out. The German trucks arrived and six hundred civilian prisoners joined the brothers as they were pushed into a train headed for Germany. Days later they arrived at the concentration camp of Amtitz.

How can I describe a concentration camp? You, child, could not picture it in your wildest nightmare. It is a place of intense suffering, great hunger, beatings, and unbearable work. The Germans wanted to eliminate the Jews, hated the religious, and felt the Poles were sub-human and not worthy of life or education. They closed the churches and schools and marched their prisoners away to extermination in "death camps."

When Father Kolbe and his brothers arrived, they saw starved prisoners wading around in the mud, sleeping on straw, struggling with vermin! They were forced to run from the train while they were beset by cruel guards attacking them with rifles and attack dogs ready to bite upon command. Daily life was one humiliation and pain after another.

Although he himself was not strong and was suffering from pneumonia, Maximilian did all he could for his fellow prisoners physically and spiritually. His faith in Mary and in God enabled him to carry on. After three months, the charges against them were found to be false, and the commander of the camp released the priest on Mary's feast day, December 8th — the Immaculate Conception!

They returned to their monastery at Niepokalanow where they found the statue of Mary laying shattered on the ground, the church ransacked, and all the furniture and their printing machines destroyed. At the request of the Polish Red Cross, the monastery was converted into a hospital which sheltered not only the wounded, but also the refugees.

After some time, Father Kolbe received permission to resume publishing his newspaper, but only one issue came off the press. On February 17, 1941 the Gestapo entered Niepokalanow. A car stopped in front and four Nazi officials got out. Although he knew they meant trouble, Father Maximilian went down to meet them. They roughly began to question his educational methods and the monastery was searched. Within an hour, Father Kolbe and four other priests were ordered into the car — arrested and accused of plotting against the authorities.

You could never imagine the sadistic brutality of the Nazi jailors toward their victims. Threats, insults, beatings, and instruments of torture were suffered by the imprisoned. Hunger, fear, and killing labor were the rule. Men looked like skeletons disguised in skin and rags! Under these difficult circumstances, it was hard to share and it was hard to care for anyone but yourself.

Yet, while in the concentration camps, Father Maximilian won the love and affection of everybody for his goodness. Boys and girls, have you noticed in your own life, it is not when all is going right that you really know a person? It is when things are rough that people show their true colors — either swine or saint! Most failed the test, but Maximilian proved to be a saint!

AP Wide World Photo

A group of children wearing concentration camp
uniforms behind barbed wire fencing at Auschwitz.

Catholic News Service

Auschwitz

9

Auschwitz

Maximilian was transferred to Auschwitz, one of the most feared camps. It was a "death factory" beyond compare! Its purpose was the extermination of Jews, Poles, and other persons or groups Hitler and the Nazis considered threatening or undesirable. In Auschwitz, there were gas chambers that could dispose of 3500 persons in 24 hours. Most prisoners were killed on arrival, but many were saved for slave labor.

Fear ruled! For some, there was a special horror of all horrors; the starvation bunker, in which prisoners received neither food nor water until death. Father Kolbe was in Auschwitz from May 28 to August 14, 1941. No one had a name — he became prisoner #16670.

Throughout his days there he tried to uplift his fellow prisoners. Ever the patriot and true Christian, he told them, "...they will not kill our souls because we prisoners are something different from our persecutors, who cannot kill in us the dignity of being Catholic and Polish... and they will never succeed in killing with fear the soul of the Polish people..."

The guards, who especially hated the religious, seemed to take special joy in tormenting him. One day he was told to load heavy wood on his shoulders and then was ordered to run. When Father Kolbe fell to the ground, he was kicked in the face and stomach and struck with a stick. He was inflicted by fifty blows and he passed out. He was thrown into the mud and covered with sticks and left there. Finally, he was transported back to the camp. He suffered many other tortures with prayer and without complaint. His holiness was recognized and many prisoners came to him after dark for confession or comfort.

Celebrating the Mass or administering the sacraments was forbidden, yet on two occasions he was able to strengthen his fellow prisoners by secretly celebrating Holy Mass and giving bits of bread for Communion.

"Hatred is not a creative force," he told his fellow prisoners. "Love alone creates. These sufferings are necessary so that those who came after us will be happy..."

His words spoke to the hearts of the suffering men. His actions, up to the very end, did bring happiness in the future, especially to one man who owes him his life.

In his last days, Maximilian never changed from the little boy who accepted the "two crowns" from the Blessed Virgin, the young student who was always ready to help his classmates, the innocent Polish boy who went to Rome. He never spoke of himself or of his sufferings. He didn't try to get easier work and always refused special treatment. Once when he was in the camp hospital, he was brought a cup of tea.

"Though it looks wonderful," he stated, "I can't take it while the others look on and don't have any."

The last week of July an incident occurred which was to shock and frighten the entire camp of Auschwitz. A prisoner from Block 14 escaped! It was the law of the camp that when this happened, as a punishment, ten men of the block would be condemned to die by starvation in the horrible underground bunker. The inmates of the camp were terrified. They were assembled in the marching field and had to stand at attention for three endless hours. When it was time for the evening meal, all prisoners, except the men in Block 14, ate. To their horror, they were forced to watch as their food was dumped into the canal. Then they were sent to bed. You can imagine the fear in their hearts as they tried to sleep that night.

The next morning the other blocks were sent to work as usual. Block 14 was lined up on the square, where they remained all day long suffering the intense July heat. Distraught by grief, burnt by thirst, exhausted by weariness, many collapsed unable to bear the suffering in their emaciated state.

Around three in the afternoon, they were given a half hour break and received the noon meal, then they were lined up again. Toward evening the other inmates returned. Tears filled their eyes at the sight they found in the yard, but they had no power to help. Finally, as night fell, the German officer, known for his cruelty, announced, "Since the fugitive has not been found, ten of you will be condemned to death."

The men, although already almost the living dead, cried out in fear. They could not bear the thought of the "starvation bunker." Their only thought was, "Dear God, don't let it be me!"

Slowly, the officer went up and down the line, picking one and bypassing another until all ten were chosen. One of them cried for his wife and his children. At this point, Father Maximilian stepped out of line. Pointing his finger toward the distraught man, he walked up to the officer.

As he eyed him, the colonel sternly questioned, "How dare you come forward. Who are you?"

"I am a Polish Catholic priest. I am old; I want to take this man's place. He has a wife and children."

The amazed officer stared at the interloper in disbelief. Then he waved his hand. "Out," he ordered the prisoner who unsteadily and tearfully returned to the line. Father Maximilian walked over and took his place. I think he finally knew what Mary's "two crowns" meant.

Everyone who witnessed this was shocked. In a place where one prisoner would refuse to give a piece of bread to another, here was someone who had offered his own life for the life of a prisoner he did not even know! In the history of Auschwitz, this was the first case where anyone had ever done such a thing.

The condemned were led away to die of starvation!

My heart aches too much to go into the details of the last days. All I will say is that it has been said that for two weeks prayers and hymns were heard coming from the cell where the usual sounds were curses, moans, and cries of despair.

On August 14, it was all over. "Raymond" received his "two crowns." The jailor entered the room, and gave those who were still alive an injection of poisonous acid. With a prayer on his lips, Father Kolbe held out his arm. Death came quietly to Father Kolbe. They tell me his face was serene and beautifully radiant.

The next day, August 15, Mary's feast of the Assumption was the day his body was taken to the ovens and burned. Father Kolbe had once said, "I would like my ashes to be scattered to the four winds and disappear without a trace." The first part of his wish was granted, but as for the second, people who knew him loved him too much to allow that to happen.

The Church now calls him Saint Maximilian Kolbe. Francis Gajowniczek and his wife Helena call him friend. They will always be grateful to the little boy who worried about being good and whose acceptance of the "two crowns" gave new life to them.

The candles around the monk's picture were blinking softly. The grandfather clock struck the half hour. Everyone was quiet. Even the adults had been paying close attention as Francis told the tale. Aunt Helena had listened with tears streaming down her apple cheeks. As she wiped them away, she sat on the side of the rocker and embraced her husband. But she couldn't speak of the story.

With a catch in her voice, she whispered, "Fran, it has stopped snowing and it is time for the children to get ready for Midnight Mass."

"Oh, Uncle Francis, we love you. Thank you for the story," cried the children together as they all reached out to hug the old man.

"And we are all happy that little Raymond grew up to be a saint. He is my hero," added Peter.

Urged by their parents to hurry, the boys and girls jumped up and searched for their coats and hats. Suddenly, they heard a little voice.

"Oh look," called Frania looking out the window. "This time I really do see the Christmas star!"

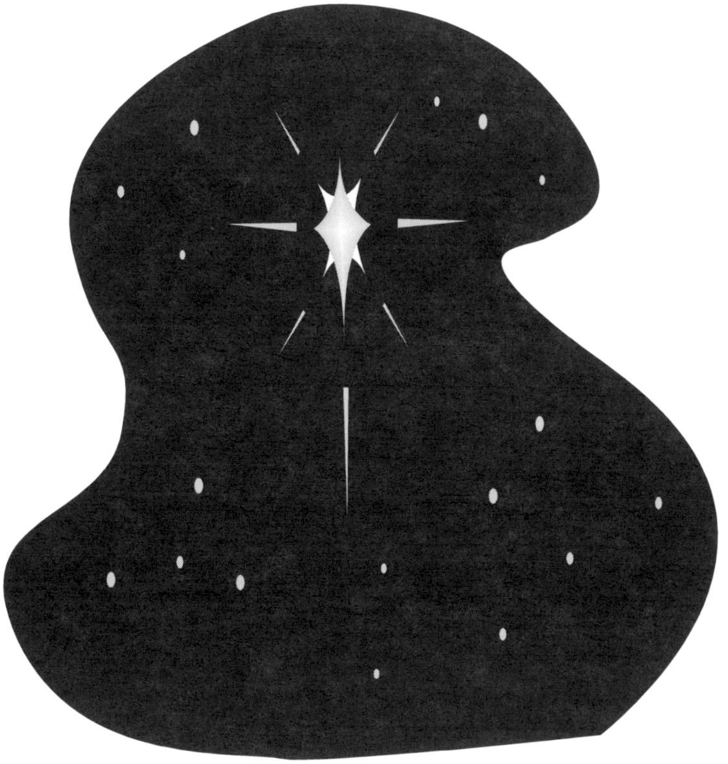

Catholic News Service

Francis Gajowniczek visits the ovens at Auschwitz, Poland.

AFTERWORD

"Love must be victorious over hate."

Francis Gajowniczek (Prisoner #5659) served in the war of 1939 as a sergeant of the Polish army. On September 28 of the same year, during the surrender of the fort of Modlin, he was taken prisoner by the Germans. He escaped, but near the Slovak border he was captured and imprisoned in Zakopane. On November 8, 1940, he was shipped to the concentration camp of Auschwitz where at the end of July 1941, he was condemned to die when a prisoner of his block escaped. He was saved by the intervention of Father Kolbe; he remained in the camp until October 25, 1944.[1]

At the moment he was spared, Grajowniczek, who did not understand German, wasn't quite sure what was happening. When he realized he was being spared by another man, he could only express with his eyes the gratitude he felt toward his savior. The rigorous camp discipline enforced silence. He stood there watching as the condemned men removed their clothing and entered their final resting place naked.

All the prisoners knew the death cell was a place of extreme suffering. They would prefer to be shot or sent to the gas chambers. They would be cruelly treated and hunger and thirst would drive them to nightmares and hallucinations.

Though the death cell had only one small barred window at the ceiling, the news leaked out how Father Kolbe maintained a contempt for death toward his captors, keeping up the spirits of the condemned who were confined to this place three meters square and empty except for a slop pail. Father Kolbe had no delirium and never complained as he grew weaker. He did his best to comfort his companions. When the jailors went to take out the corpses, he was most often found standing or kneeling, praying or singing a hymn, repeated by the chorus around him.[2]

When he was freed from the concentration camp in 1945, Gajowniczek went to the Franciscan Monastery at Niepokalanow, which Father Kolbe had founded, to tell the story of Kolbe's heroic act. He traveled all over the world to tell the story of Father Kolbe's sacrifice to all who would listen. He was at St. Peter's Basilica in 1971 when Father Kolbe was beatified in Rome and again in 1982, when Father Kolbe was formally declared Saint Maximilian Kolbe.[3]

After his deliverance, Francis lived with his wife Helena in a little house near Pstrowski Street in Brzeg (B'zhe'g), Poland. He kept a little shrine to Maximilian Maria Kolbe in a place of honor in his living room. Mr. Gajowniczek was an active member of the Union of Political Prisoners, then the Association of Fighters for Liberty and Democracy. He had hoped to live to see the day when shooting would stop in all corners of the world and lawlessness and brutality disappear.[4] Francis died on March 13, 1995 at 94 years of age.

1. St. Maximilian Kolbe: Ricciardi, Antonio
2. Forget Not Love: Frossard, Andre
3. Polish Biographical Dictionary
4. Newspaper Interview of Francis Gajowniczek 1971

"...today you need no longer hesitate to use the word 'saints': think of Father Maximilian Kolbe who was starved and finally murdered by an injection of carbolic acid at Auschwitz and who in 1983 was canonized... you may ask whether we really need to refer to "saints." Wouldn't it suffice just to refer to "decent" people? It is true that they form a minority. More than that, they will always remain a minority. And yet I see therein the very challenge to join the minority. For the world is in a bad state. But everything will become still worse unless each of us does his best."

—Viktor E. Frankl

"There will be sufferings, temptations; perhaps you will be haunted by discouragement... learn to be ready for the greatest sacrifices... do not desire extraordinary things, but simply to perform the will of the Immaculata..."

— St. Maximilian Kolbe

CHRONOLOGY

1894	January 8 – born in Zdunska-Wola, Poland
1903	May (approximate date) – vision of Blessed Virgin
1907	Easter – called to be a student at Franciscan seminary
	October – entered Franciscan community
1910	September 4 – entered novitiate, now Friar Maximilian
1911	September 5 – first vows
1912	October 28 – left Poland to study in Rome
1914	August – father hanged during World War I
	November 1 – solemn perpetual vows
1917	October 16 – consecrated to Mary – founded *The Militia Immaculatae*
1918	April 28 – ordained priest
	April 29 – said first Mass
1920	August 11 – sent to sanatorium for tuberculosis
1922	January – began publishing magazine, *The Knight of the Immaculata*
1927	April 13 – left sanatorium
	October 1 – named Superior of Niepokalanow
1930	February 26 – left for Far East
	December 3 – brother Joseph (Father Alphonse) died
	April 24 – arrived in Nagasaki
1933	*The Knight* published in Japanese
1936	May 26 – returned to Poland due to poor health
1937	December 8 – went on radio for first time
1939	September 1 – Germany attacked Poland
	September 16 – arrested
	September 24 – arrived in Amtitz concentration camp
	December – freed – returned to Nicpokalanow
1941	February 17 – rearrested by Germans
	May 28 – sent to Auschwitz
	July 31 – offered his life for another prisoner
	August 14 – died in starvation bunker
	August 15 – body burned in Auschwitz crematorium
1943	Brother Francis died in concentration camp at Buchenwald
1946	March 17 – mother died at age seventy-six
1971	Beatified in Rome
1982	October 10 – Pope John Paul II declared Maximilian a saint and added his name to the Canon of Saints of the Church

GLOSSARY

abscess – accumulation of pus in a body tissue.

abolish – to do away with a law; to put an end to.

admiral – the commander–in–chief of a fleet of ships.

affection – devotion or love.

appointment – a mutual agreement for a meeting.

authorities – persons having legal power.

bosom – the breast of a human being.

bunker – a partially underground chamber built as a shelter or
    prison.

campaign – a military operation.

canal – an artificial waterway.

capture – to take by force.

captor – a person who has captured another person.

carp – fish found in the Balkan Sea

chapel – a private place of prayer; a small church.

chirp – short sharp sounds made by small birds.

chorus – group of persons singing together.

civilian – a person not on active duty in the military.

compassion – a feeling of deep sympathy and sorrow.

concentration camp – a guarded compound for confinement for the
    persecution of prisoners.

congregation – a group of people brought together for religious
    worship.

consecrate – to declare sacred; dedicate to the service of God.

console – to give solace or comfort.

contemplate – to observe thoughtfully.

contempt – a feeling of distain for something mean or vile; scorn.

convent – a community of women in religious life.

corpse – a dead body.

courageous – a state of being brave.

crown – a type of headware often made of precious metal and gems.

cruel – willfully causing pain or distress on others.

curse – an obscene word used in anger or despair.

dedicate – to set apart and consecrate to God.
delirium – a temporary disturbance of consciousness marked by
    hallucinations.
destined – bound to be or do something.
destiny – something that is to happen to a particular person.
dignity – manner indicating self–respect.
disbelief – refusal to believe.
distraught – bewildered; deeply agitated.
dowry – money that a wife brings to her husband at marriage;
    money needed by a young girl to enter the convent.

elders – people of greater age; older.
emaciated – gradual wasting away of flesh.
endure – to bear patiently.
enthusiastic – eager; lively; great interest.
eventually – finally; at some later date.
evil – wicked; harmful.
extermination – to get rid of by destroying.

fascinated – to arouse the interest of; to transfix.
fathom – to comprehend or understand.
fiery – easily angered.
frontier – the part of a country that borders another country.
fugitive – a person who is fleeing from difficult circumstances.
furrowed – to make wrinkles in the face.

glimmering – shining faintly.
glisten – to reflect a sparkling light.
gwiazdka – in the Polish language, the little star, the Christmas star.

hallucination – a sensory experience of something that does not
    exist outside the mind.
hemorrhage – to bleed profusely.
howl – a mournful cry.
humiliation – a loss of self–respect, pride, or dignity.

incident – an occurrence or event.
independence – not influenced or controlled by others.
inflict – to impose anything unwelcome.
injection – a liquid forced into the body by needle.

inspire – to influence; to give confidence.

intense – great in force.

interloper – someone who thrusts himself into the affairs of another.

intervening – coming between.

intervention – the act of interfering in another's affairs.

jail – a prison

jailor – a person who is in charge of a section of a jail.

loom – an apparatus for weaving fabric.

manger – a box in a stable from which animals eat.

missionary – a person sent out by a church to spread its religion in a foreign country.

monastery – a place where a group of monks live.

monk – a man who has joined a religious order whose members live together according to certain rules, after vowing to give up worldly goods, never to marry, etc.

mystery – something hard to explain or solve.

Nazi – having to do with the fascist political party that ruled Germany under Hitler from 1933 to 1945.

novitiate – the preparation time before becoming a nun, monk, or other religious.

obstinate – stubborn; not willing to change.

oplatwk – in Poland, the wafer shared on Christmas Eve.

ornament – decoration.

parlor – old fashioned living room.

patriotic – showing great love for one's country.

pawns – a chess piece of lowest rank.

permanently – lasting for a very long time.

persecutor – one who treats others in a harsh way.

persevere – to keep doing something in spite of difficulty.

pharmacist – a person trained to prepare and sell drugs according to a doctor's orders.

pharmacy – a drugstore.

plaguing – to trouble or make suffer.

plump – chubby.

pneumonia – a condition in which the lungs become inflamed.

ponder – to think deeply about something.

prosperity – the condition of being prosperous, wealthy, or successful.

publish – to prepare and bring out for sale a book, magazine, or newspaper.

ransack – to search thoroughly in order to rob or plunder.

religious sister – a member of a community of nuns.

rigorous – severe or harsh.

rivulet – a little stream.

sacrifice – the act of giving up one thing for the sake of something else.

sadistic – getting pleasure from hurting others.

sanatarium – a quiet rest home for people getting over a serious ailment.

seminary – a school where priests are trained.

severe – harsh or stern; hard to bear.

shelter – to protect.

shivering – to shake or tremble from fear or cold.

slop pot – a pot for holding liquid waste; in this case, a pot used as a toilet.

souvenir – an article given in remembrance of a place visited.

sparkling – glistening; glittering;

spellbound – fascinated; enchanted.

spiteful – deliberately annoying.

squirming – twisting and turning.

startled – frightened or surprised.

Superior – the head of a monastery or convent.

supper – the last meal of the day, eaten in the evening.

surrender – to give oneself up, especially as a prisoner.

swine – a mean or disgusting person.

switch – a thin twig or stick used for whipping.

tavern – a place where beer, whiskey, etc. are sold and drunk.

technology – a method of dealing with a technical problem; science put to use in a practical way.

tormenting – to make suffer in body or mind.

traditions – a custom or belief handed down by word of mouth.

trance – the state of being conscious, but unable to move or act; being completely lost in thought.

translate – to put into words of a different language.

tuberculosis – a disease in which the lungs or tissue waste away.

tutor – a teacher who teaches one student at a time; a private teacher.

unite – to join together to make one.

vermin – small animals or insects, such as rats or flies, that cause harm or are troublesome to people.

victim – someone killed, hurt, sacrificed, or destroyed.

victory – the winning of a battle.

vision – something seen in one's mind or while in a trance.

wigilia – in Poland, the Christmas Eve supper.

Further Reading

Frossard, Andre. *Forget Not Love.* Ignatius Press, San Francisco, CA; 1991

Frankl, Viktor. *Man's Search For Meaning.* Simon & Schuster, Inc., New York, NY; 1984

Ricciardi, Antonio. *St. Maximilian Kolbe.* Daughters of St. Paul, Boston, MA; 1982

McSheffery, Rev. Daniel F. *Raymond Kolbe – Modern Martyr.*

——— About the Author ———

CLAIRE JORDAN MOHAN, formerly of King of Prussia and Lansdale, now resides in Chalfont, Pennsylvania with her husband, Robert. Having retired from full-time teaching at Visitation B.V.M. School in Trooper, PA, she spends her time writing, traveling and enjoying her grandchildren. She is a CCD teacher at her parish and has been a tutor at Graterford Prison.

She has had many articles published in magazines and newspapers and has appeared on national radio and television shows, including Mother Angelica Live, the 700 Club, and CNBC. On a trip to Rome for the Beatification of Blessed Frances Siedliska, Claire Mohan presented a special edition of her book *"A Red Rose for Frania"* to Pope John Paul II. Her recent book *"The Young Life of Pope John Paul II"* was also hand-delivered to Our Holy Father.

She is the mother of five children and grandmother of twelve. Claire is a graduate of Little Flower High School and is a 1984 summa cum laude graduate of Villanova University where she was valedictorian of her class. She attended Chestnut Hill College and West Chester University for graduate studies. Claire Jordan Mohan welcomes interviews and speaking engagements.

Other Books

by Claire Jordan Mohan

A Red Rose for Frania

This children's book offers young readers a thoughtful endearing story of Frances Siedliska's joys and struggles on her pathway to sainthood. This story demonstrates courage and perseverance as it describes Frania's poor health and obstacles in committing to religious life.

Kaze's True Home

This delightful story of the young life of Maria Kaupas will inspire each child as young Casimira follows her star to attain "the impossible dream." "Kaze" as she was called, was neither wealthy nor did she enjoy the opportunities of the young people of today, but she loved God and was able to share her love with others.
$14.95 hardcover

The Young Life of Pope John Paul II

Young and old will enjoy this story which details the young life of Pope John Paul II while a boy in Poland. The way Karol Wojtyla handles the triumphs of his life will inspire children to emulate this courageous boy. They learn his life was just like theirs — a mixture of sadness and joy. They meet "a real boy" who shares their hobbies and interests and in the end, grows up to be a most respected religious and world leader. *$14.95 hardcover $7.95 paperback*

The Young Life of Mother Teresa of Calcutta

How Gonxha Agnes Bojaxhiu grew to be a world famous personage and a living example of Jesus in a dark world is the basis for this new book for young and old to treasure. This story gives insight into the people and events in Mother Teresa's young life that shaped the final woman — the early death of her beloved father, Nikola, a political figure in the days of unrest of Yugoslavia; — her mother, the warm hospitable Dronda, who always had time for others. We learn how a "pretty mischievous young tomboy" eventually became a world revered "living saint."
$14.95 hardcover $7.95 paperback

—————— Other Books ——————
continued

Give Me Jesus

Give Me Jesus is a book for everyone, no matter what the age. The selections compiled by the author touch the heart. It may be used simply to inspire or it may be a tool in giving children building blocks to faith. It contains biblical stories juxtaposed with modern day experiences; it presents well-loved prayers interspersed with delightful thoughts and poems from the anonymous to the famous writer. You will smile; you will cry; you will pray as you peruse its pages. It has been called "magical."
$7.95 paperback

Available at your local bookstore or order direct from Young Sparrow Press.

Send your check or money order, including $3.00 shipping for one copy, and 50¢ for each additional copy to:
Young Sparrow Press, P.O. Box 265, Worcester, PA 19490

—What Others Are Saying...—

About... *Kaze's True Home*

"We live in an era rampant with violence, hate, and fear where the media gives the impression that everyone is corrupt and evil. It is very refreshing to read a story about a contemporary who is a real live saint. A ray of sunshine in a dark world! A marvelous job!" — *Peter A. Mankas, Director, Lansdale Public Library, Lansdale, PA*

"I enjoyed reading the book. I found it interesting, and exciting to follow Casimira on her journeys' — though it also made me cry." — *Rachel Galie, Visitation BVM School, Trooper, PA*

About... *The Young Life of Pope John Paul II*

"...a delightful read for children... leads the reader into the very soul of that deeply introspective and brilliant young man." — *Catholic Library Association*

"...this is a splendid little book. Children will enjoy it at home and from the school library." — *The Upper Peninsula Catholic*

About... *The Young Life of Mother Teresa of Calcutta*

"...not only a pleasant introduction to Mother Teresa... but also an inspiring introduction to the life and works of all missionaries... The love and compassion shown in Mother Teresa's quotation will strengthen everyone who reads them." —*Catholic Library Association*

"Here is a lovely book written for children about Mother Teresa... packed with beautiful images to provoke our imagination." — *T.O.R.C.H. Book Reviews*

About... *Give Me Jesus*

"I really like this book." — *Heather Hinkle, Twin Oaks Elementary School*

"This collection is broad and embracing, touching a variety of inner worlds. It is colorful, playful, intimate, and expressive... As an editor, I find this work delightful." — *Kass Dotterweich, Liguori Publications*

"This book of prayers for children is very inspiring. It presents poems for enjoyment and memorization — a delight!" — *Theresa Johnson, Catholic Heritage Curricula*

— What Others Are Saying —
— About Maximilian Kolbe —

"I loved this story! ...Learned some things as well." — *Margaret F. McMenamin, CCD Coordinator, St. Jude School, Chalfont, PA*

"I never really heard of St. Maximilian Kolbe before reading this book... when I first learned of him, I thought he was as old as Jesus, but as I read on, I found out he lived during World War II. It's a kind of book you can get your nose in and you can't take it out." — *John Milko, Fourth Grade, Pine Run Elementary School, Doylestown, PA*

"...This book was one of my favorites, and I advise everyone who loves to read to take a look at it. The facts poured out, with fun twists to them. I learned so much about a great leader and I enjoyed every page of this book." — *Drew Wilkens, Fifth Grade, Pine Run Elementary School, Doylestown, PA*

"...As a person of Polish descent, I found this story inspirational. In a world filled with intolerance, St. Maximilian Kolbe was a wonderful example of acceptance. Hopefully, all those who read this story will model their lives after him." — *Loretta J. Halas, Teacher Grade 7, Cedarbrook Middle School, Elkins Park, PA*

"...I liked this book a lot. The one thing I really liked was the way the author wrote the story of Maximilian Kolbe through the eyes of the man he saved. I thought St. Maximilian was very brave in giving his life for someone he didn't even know." — *Kristen Gallagher, Seventh Grade, Richboro Middle School, Richboro, PA*

"This is a great story. As my grandmother read it to us, I listened to every word and never moved until the end. I found St. Maximilian to be a great hero. I really admire him." — *Susannah Mohan, Sixth Grade, Montgomery County Magnet School, Rockville, MD*